to horse around
to play in a rowdy way

monkey business
silly behavior

THERE'S A FROG IN MY THROAT!
440 Animal Sayings a Little Bird Told Me

written by
Loreen Leedy & Pat Street

illustrated by
Loreen Leedy

lucky duck
fortunate person

Holiday House
New York

meow!

It's the cat's meow!
It's terrific!

dear reader,

to turn turtle
to turn upside down

We love animal sayings! Sayings pack a lot of meaning into a few words. Plus, it's just more fun to say "It's raining cats and dogs" than "It's raining hard."

Every language has its own unique sayings. For this book, we collected 440 of our favorite animal sayings in English. As you will see, many of them compare people to animals.

A **simile** makes a comparison using the word *like* or the word *as*. If someone is "as quiet as a mouse," that person is silent. (Mice aren't noisy.)

A **metaphor** also makes a comparison, but without *like* or *as*. If someone is a "night owl," he or she likes to stay up late. (Owls are active at night.)

An **idiom** doesn't mean exactly what the words say. For example, "She has butterflies in her stomach" doesn't mean she's eaten some butterflies! Instead, it means "She feels nervous."

A **proverb** gives advice about how to act in daily life. For example, to advise someone not to exaggerate a problem, you can say, "Don't make a mountain out of a molehill."

We fit as many animal sayings into these pages as we could—even a few about feathers and shells and fur and tails. Most of these sayings are well known, but we think some will be new to you. We included one common meaning for each saying. (Some have more than one meaning.)

Happy reading! We hope you will enjoy this book "till the cows come home"—for a very long time!

See you later, alligator!
Loreen Leedy and Pat Street

It's not a fit night out for man or beast.
The weather is terrible.

I killed two birds with one stone.
I got two things done with one action.

woolgathering
daydreaming

2

contents

We're off like a herd of turtles.
We're getting a slow start.

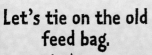

Let's tie on the old feed bag.
Let's eat.

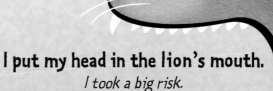

What's the buzz?
What are people saying?

It's the bee's knees!
It's terrific!

I put my head in the lion's mouth.
I took a big risk.

3

This place is going to the dogs.
Things are getting worse and worse.

dog-eared page
folded page corner

Let sleeping dogs lie.
Leave old problems alone.

Stop hounding me!
Stop pestering me!

Hot dog!
Wow!

You're barking up the wrong tree.
You've got the wrong idea.

You can't teach an old dog new tricks.
It's harder for an older person to learn new things.

His bark is worse than his bite.
He's not as fierce as he seems.

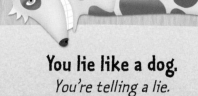

It's a dog-eat-dog world.
Life can be brutally competitive.

You lie like a dog.
You're telling a lie.

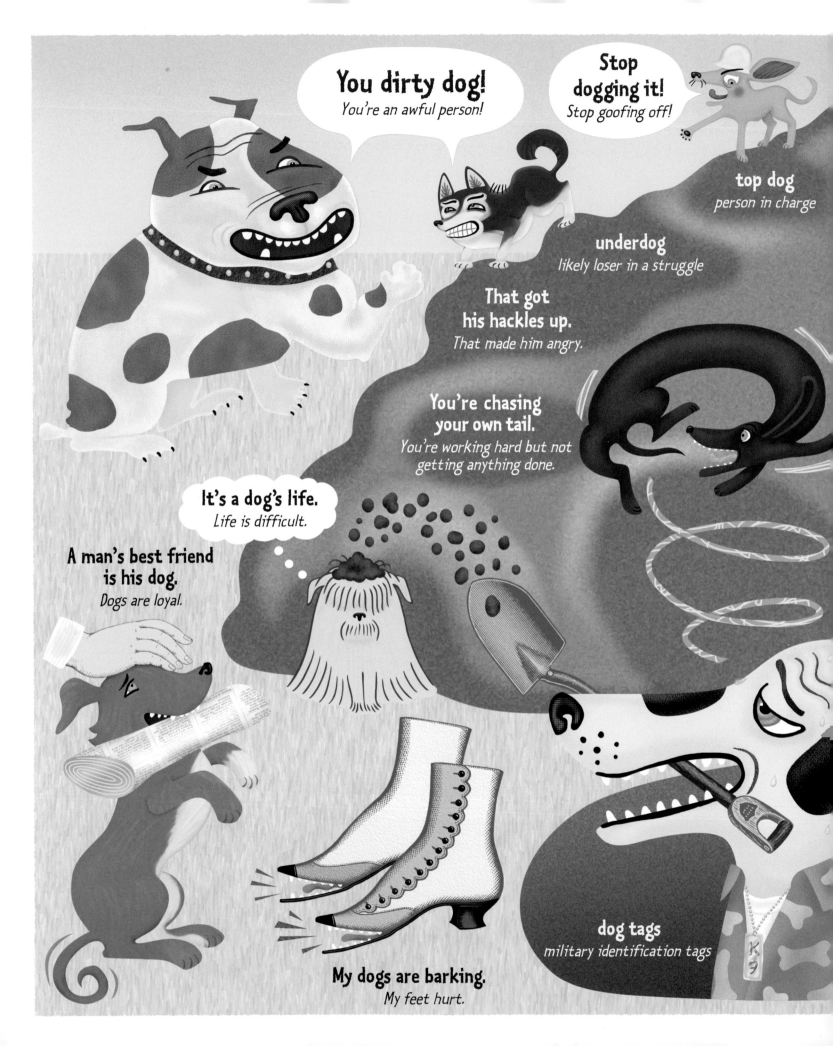

The tail is wagging the dog. *A small part is controlling the whole thing.*

They fight like cats and dogs. *They have fierce arguments.*

They put on a dog-and-pony show. *They gave us a fancy sales pitch.*

The fur is going to fly. *There will be a big fight.*

to do the doggie paddle *to swim like a dog*

It's a three-dog night. *It's very cold.*

It's raining cats and dogs. *It's raining hard.*

8

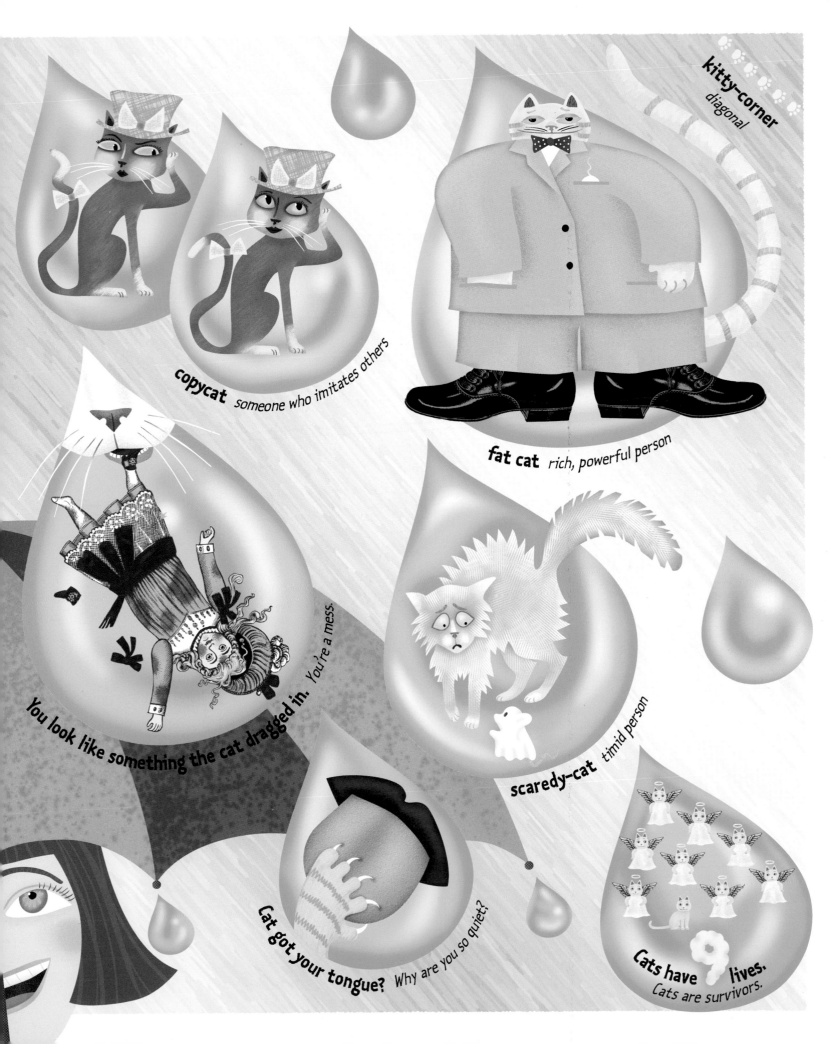

copycat *someone who imitates others*

kitty-corner *diagonal*

fat cat *rich, powerful person*

You look like something the cat dragged in. *You're a mess.*

scaredy-cat *timid person*

Cat got your tongue? *Why are you so quiet?*

Cats have 9 lives. *Cats are survivors.*

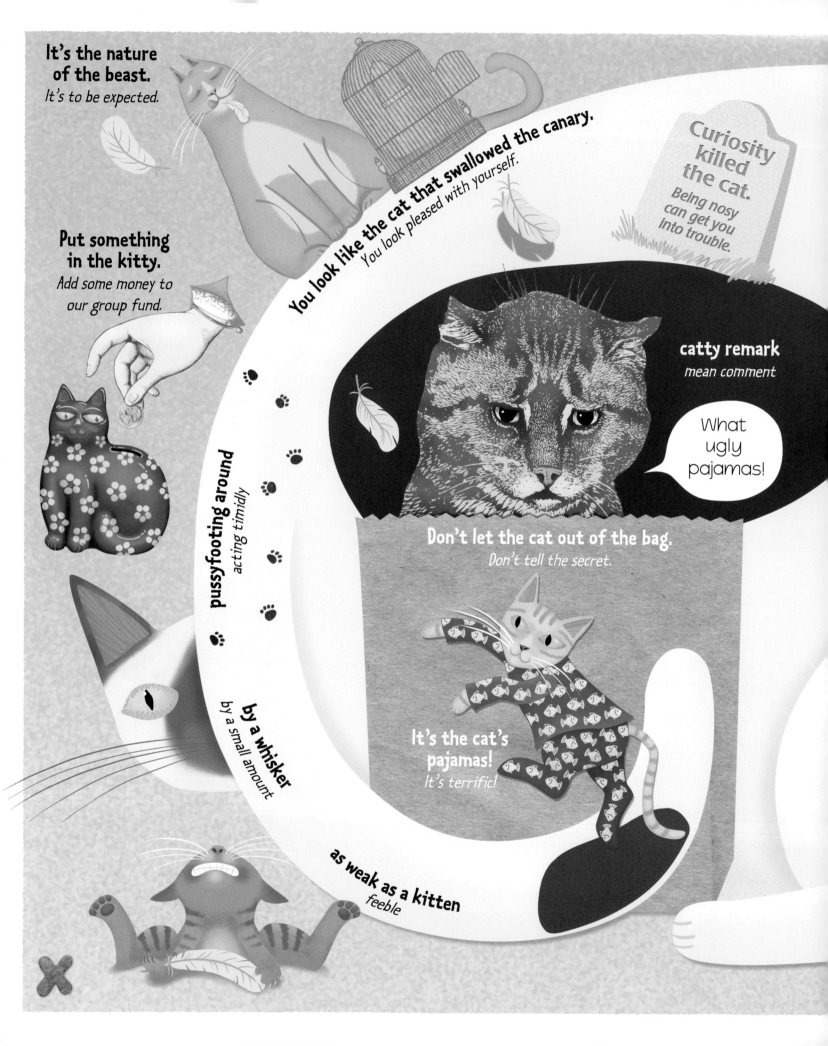

It's the nature of the beast.
It's to be expected.

Put something in the kitty.
Add some money to our group fund.

You look like the cat that swallowed the canary.
You look pleased with yourself.

Curiosity killed the cat.
Being nosy can get you into trouble.

catty remark
mean comment

What ugly pajamas!

pussyfooting around
acting timidly

Don't let the cat out of the bag.
Don't tell the secret.

by a whisker
by a small amount

It's the cat's pajamas!
It's terrific!

as weak as a kitten
feeble

When the cat's away, the mice will play.
Workers goof off when the boss is gone.

Are you a man or a mouse?
Are you brave or cowardly?

as quiet as a mouse
silent

Who will bell the cat?
Who will face danger for the good of us all?

to build a better mousetrap
to invent or improve a product

to play cat and mouse
to cruelly toy with someone

catnap
short period of sleep

mouse potato
frequent computer user

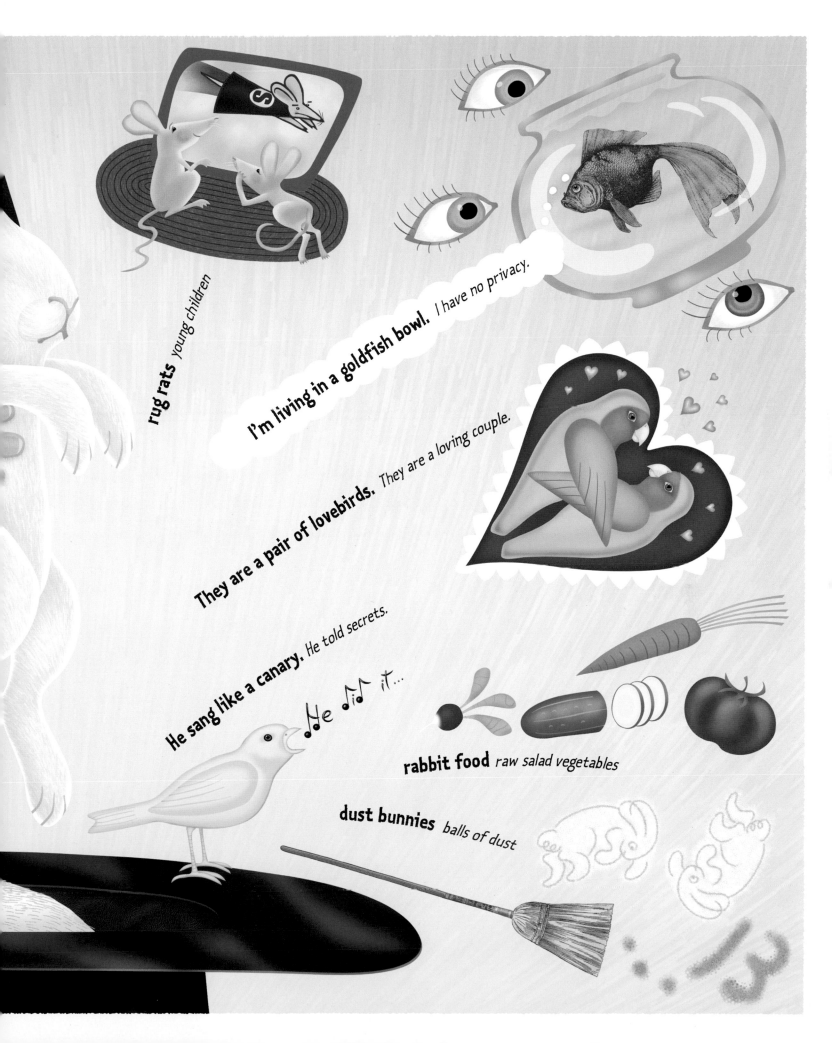

rug rats young children

I'm living in a goldfish bowl. I have no privacy.

They are a pair of lovebirds. They are a loving couple.

He sang like a canary. He told secrets.

He did it...

rabbit food raw salad vegetables

dust bunnies balls of dust

I don't want to hear another peep out of you!
Be quiet!

There's nobody here but us chickens.
We're the only ones here.

You're letting the fox guard the henhouse.
You're putting the wrong person in charge.

Peep!

as mad as a wet hen
furious

She gets up with the chickens.
She wakes up early in the morning.

She is first in the pecking order.
She has the top rank in our group.

chicken feed
small amount of money

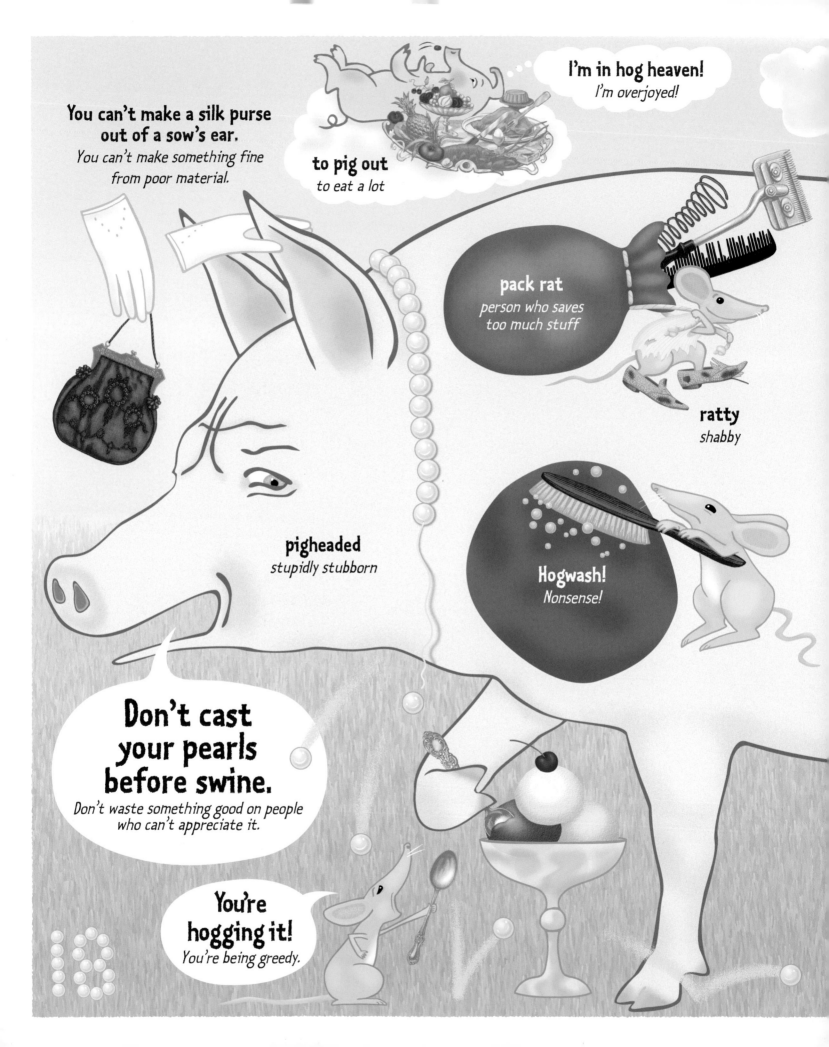

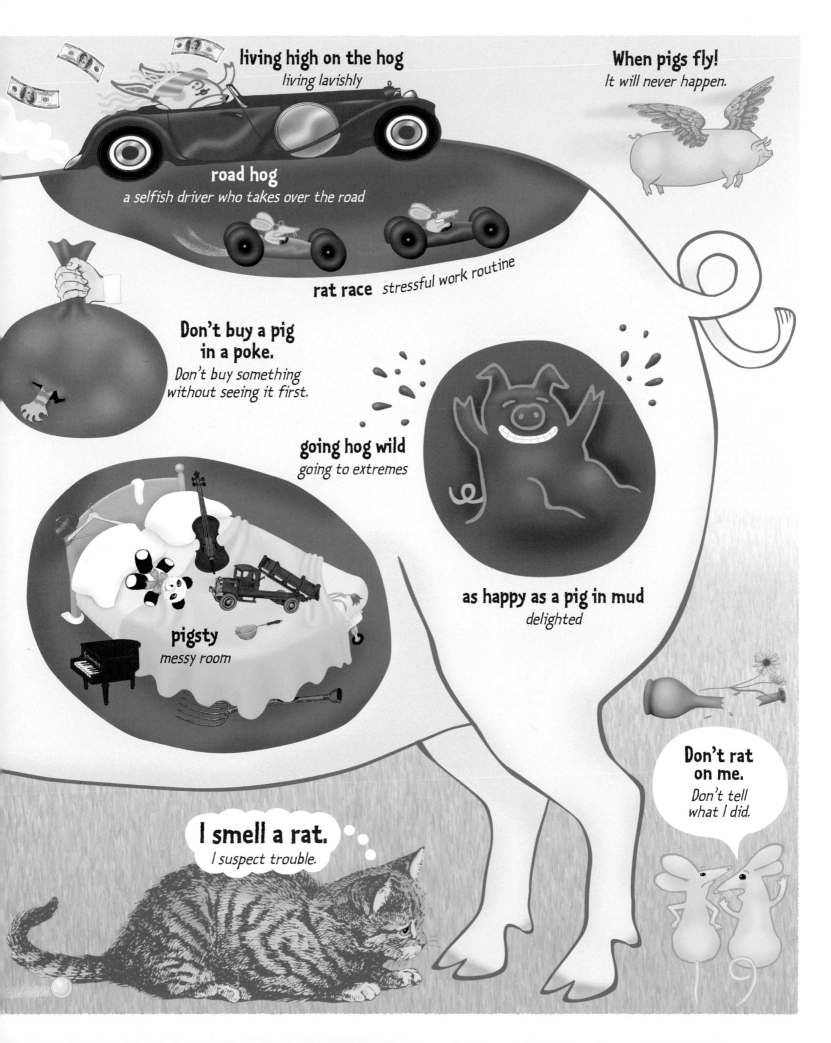

Get off your high horse.
Stop acting superior.

charley horse
leg cramp

We have to hoof it.
We have to walk.

That's a horse of a different color.
That's something else entirely.

Hold your horses!
Be patient!

It's from horse-and-buggy days.
It's old-fashioned.

You can lead a horse to water, but you can't make him drink.
You can't force someone to take advice.

It's straight from the horse's mouth.
I heard it directly from someone who was there.

I could eat a horse.
I'm very hungry.

Horsefeathers!
Nonsense!

21

It's like waving a red flag in front of a bull.
It's something that will make him very angry.

Were you raised in a barn?
You are so rude!

He's like a bull in a china shop.
He's very clumsy.

cash cow
profitable business

I'm on the horns of a dilemma.
I have to make a tough choice.

as dark as the inside of a cow
pitch-black

cowlick
tuft of hair that sticks out

bullheaded
obstinate

Big hat, no cattle.
He is pretending to be a big shot.

Take the bull by the horns.
Tackle the problem.

That was a bull's-eye!
You hit the target!

It's a sacred cow.
We can't change it.

He's a wolf in sheep's clothing.
He's an enemy pretending to be a friend.

as innocent as a lamb
blameless

scapegoat
innocent person who gets blamed

She pulled the wool over his eyes.
She fooled him.

Separate the sheep from the goats.
Divide the good from the bad.

to butt heads
to argue fiercely

That will get his goat.
That will make him angry.

in two shakes of a lamb's tail
quickly

sheepish
embarrassed

to butt in
to intrude

Butt out!
Mind your own business!

to get fleeced
to be swindled

23

That's just ducky!
That's just great!

Get your ducks in a row.
Get organized.

Quack!

If it looks like a duck, walks like a duck, and quacks like a duck, it's a DUCK!
It's obvious!

DUCKS
GEESE

goose egg
zero

We're dead ducks.
We're going to lose.

There's a frog in my throat!
My throat is hoarse!

Ribbet!

What's sauce for the goose is sauce for the gander.
If you can do it, so can I.

My goose is cooked.
I'm in trouble.

odd duck
peculiar person

24k

Don't kill the goose that lays the golden eggs.
Don't destroy the source of your good fortune.

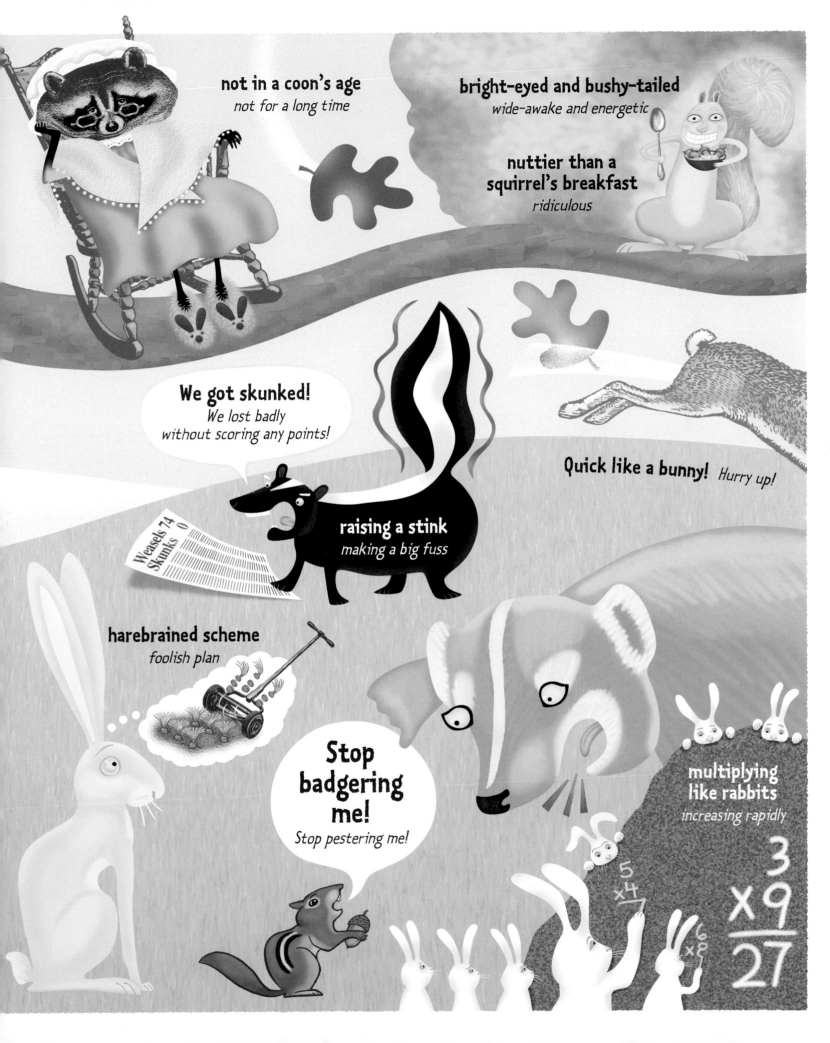

She fawns on him.
She slavishly tries to please him.

wolfing down food
eating too fast

Put a tail on him.
Send a spy to follow him secretly.

He's a lone wolf.
He likes to be alone.

Grrrrr!

to lock horns
to disagree

What are your demands?

Unfair!

cub reporter
journalist who is new on the job

wildcat strike
unauthorized work stoppage

to keep the wolf from the door
to provide food for one's family

She threw me to the wolves.
She abandoned me in a bad situation.

He is crazy like a fox.
He seems foolish, yet he is outsmarting everyone.

as sly as a fox
clever

?

dumb bunny
stupid person

eager beaver
enthusiastic person

busy beaver
hard worker

29

I've seen the elephant.
I've seen more than enough.

When you hear hoofbeats, think horses, not zebras.
Try the simple solution first.

Don't bury your head in the sand like an ostrich.
Don't hide from reality.

They have the herd instinct.
They follow the crowd.

There's an elephant in the room.
There's a big problem nobody wants to face.

white elephant
fancy thing no one wants

She has a memory like an elephant.
She won't forget.

The leopard can't change his spots.
A person's nature will stay the same.

zebra crossing
striped crosswalk

It's an 800-pound gorilla.
It's an uncontrollable problem.

It's more fun than a barrel of monkeys.
It's very enjoyable.

as brave as a lion
courageous

to lionize someone
to treat someone like a celebrity

the lion's share
the biggest portion

to laugh like a hyena
laughing loudly

Ha! Ha! Ha!

Don't let the camel get its nose under the tent.
Don't let something bad get started.

I have a tiger by the tail.
This problem is huge.

He is a paper tiger.
He seems strong, but he is actually weak.

monkeyshines
mischievous tricks

to go ape
to act wildly

grease monkey
mechanic

It threw a monkey wrench into our plans.
It ruined our plans.

They made a monkey out of me.
They made me look foolish.

monkey suit
tuxedo

monkey see, monkey do
to copy what other people do

kangaroo court
a court that ignores the law

It's a dinosaur.
It's out of date.

It's neither fish nor fowl.
It doesn't fit easily into any category.

fossil
old person or thing

on the WING

bird's-eye view
view from overhead

Keep an eagle eye on it.
Watch it carefully.

round-robin
project that's completed as different people add to it step-by-step

I'm as free as a bird.
There's nothing I have to do right now.

It's as light as a feather. *It weighs very little.*

You could've knocked me down with a feather.
I was very surprised.

Birds of a feather flock together.
Similar people stick together.

I was sent on a wild-goose chase.
I was asked to search for something that couldn't be found.

Don't ruffle any feathers.
Don't upset anyone.

stool pigeon
police informer

just for a lark *just for fun*

cheerful
as happy as a lark

to wing it
to improvise

crow's-feet
wrinkles in the corners of the eyes

I had to eat crow.
I had to admit I was wrong.

crow's nest
lookout platform

as the crow flies *in a straight line*

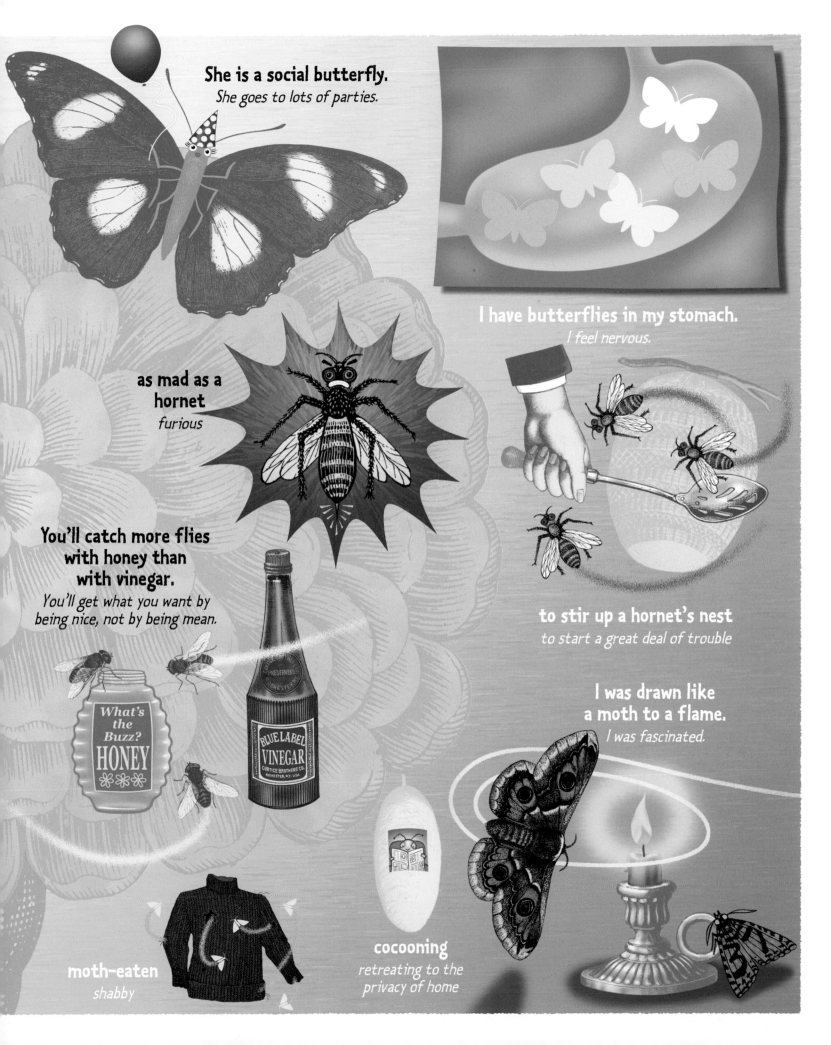

She is a social butterfly.
She goes to lots of parties.

I have butterflies in my stomach.
I feel nervous.

as mad as a hornet
furious

You'll catch more flies with honey than with vinegar.
You'll get what you want by being nice, not by being mean.

What's the Buzz? HONEY

BLUE LABEL VINEGAR
CURTICE BROTHERS CO.
ROCHESTER, N.Y. USA

to stir up a hornet's nest
to start a great deal of trouble

I was drawn like a moth to a flame.
I was fascinated.

moth-eaten
shabby

cocooning
retreating to the privacy of home

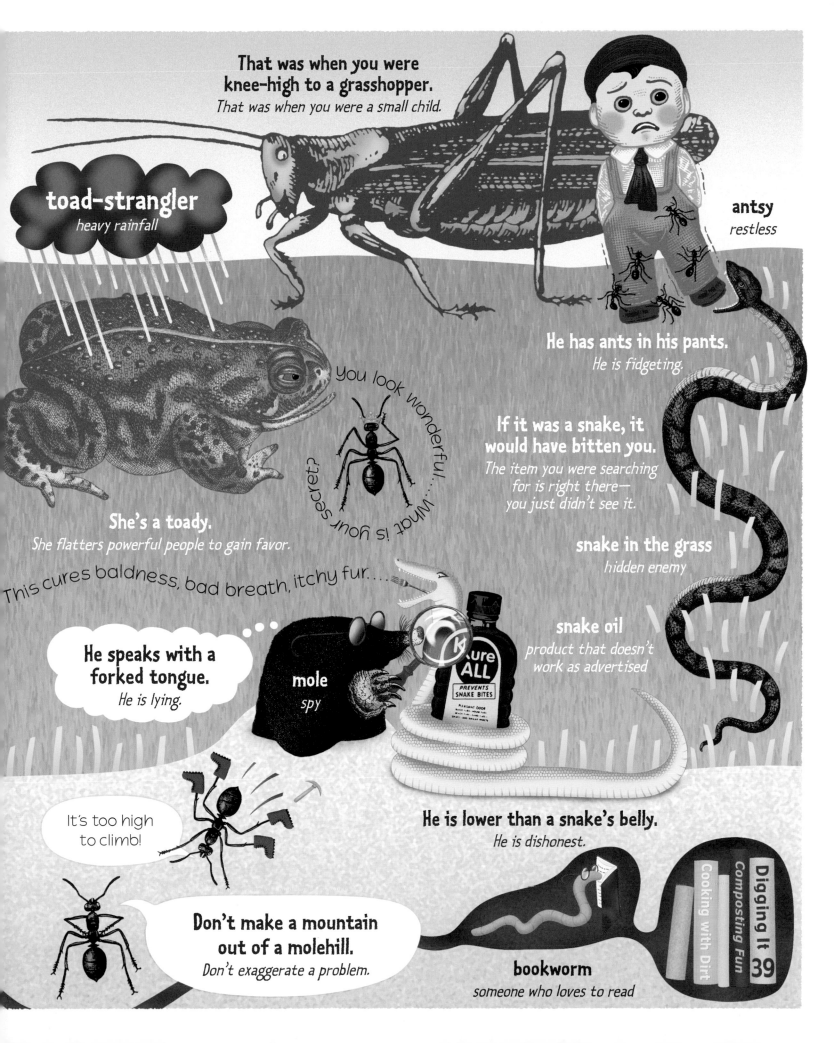

That was when you were
knee-high to a grasshopper.
That was when you were a small child.

antsy
restless

toad-strangler
heavy rainfall

He has ants in his pants.
He is fidgeting.

You look wonderful.....What is your secret?

If it was a snake, it
would have bitten you.
*The item you were searching
for is right there—
you just didn't see it.*

She's a toady.
She flatters powerful people to gain favor.

snake in the grass
hidden enemy

This cures baldness, bad breath, itchy fur.....

snake oil
*product that doesn't
work as advertised*

He speaks with a
forked tongue.
He is lying.

mole
spy

ure
ALL
PREVENTS
SNAKE BITES

It's too high
to climb!

He is lower than a snake's belly.
He is dishonest.

Don't make a mountain
out of a molehill.
Don't exaggerate a problem.

Digging It
39
Composting Fun
Cooking with Dirt

bookworm
someone who loves to read

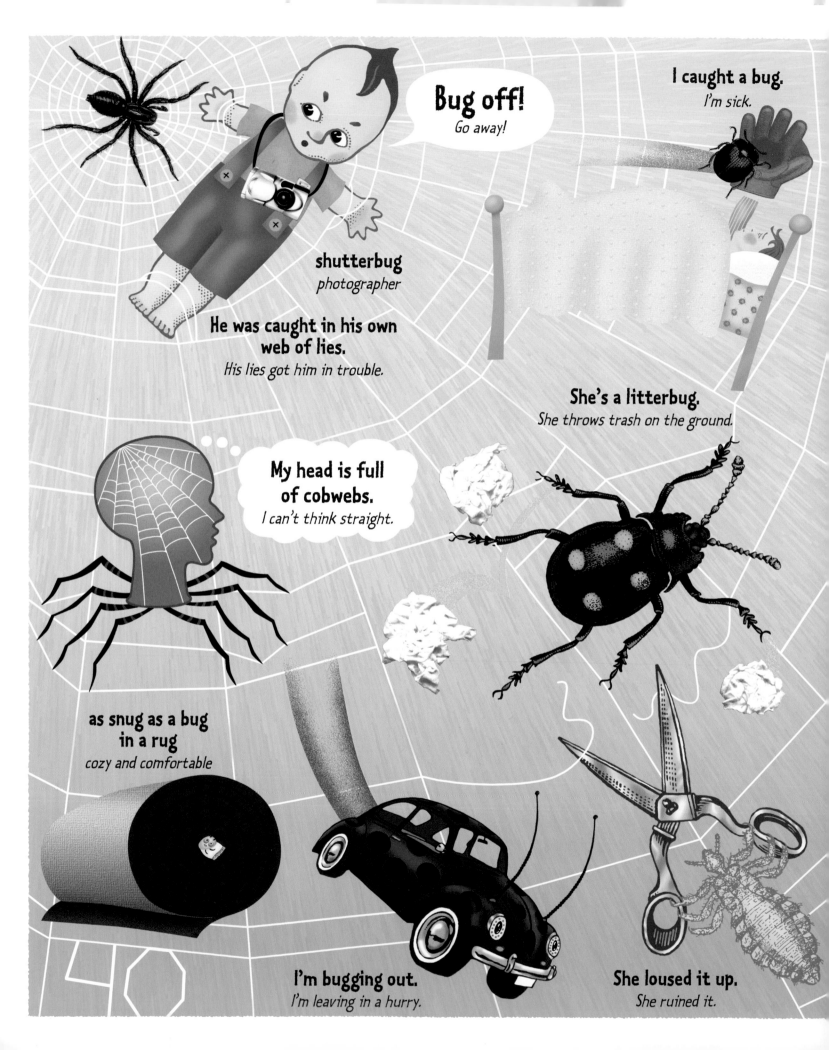

I feel like a fish out of water.
I feel out of place.

See you later, alligator!
Good-bye for now!

to cry crocodile tears
to pretend to be sorry

under the WAVES

Something smells fishy.
I suspect wrongdoing.

This is a fine kettle of fish.
This is a predicament.

You're smart.

You're pretty.

Poor me.

You're nice.

You're sweet.

She is fishing for compliments.
She is trying to get praise.

to flounder around
to fumble and struggle

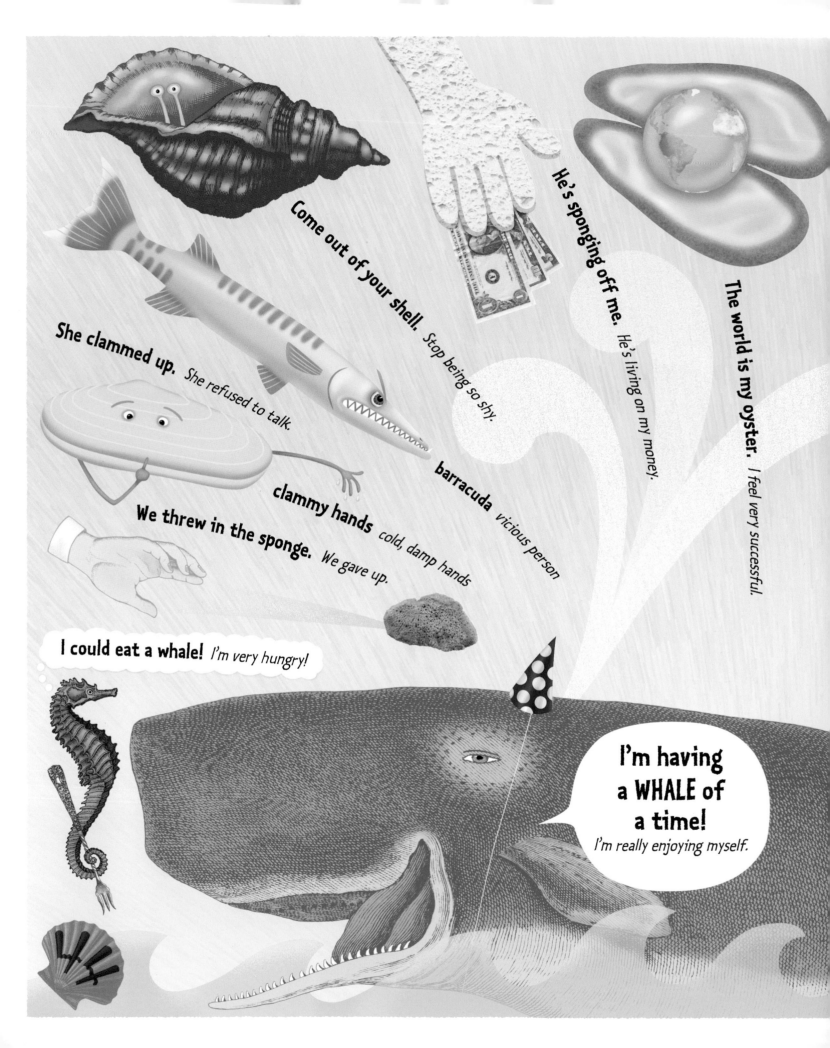

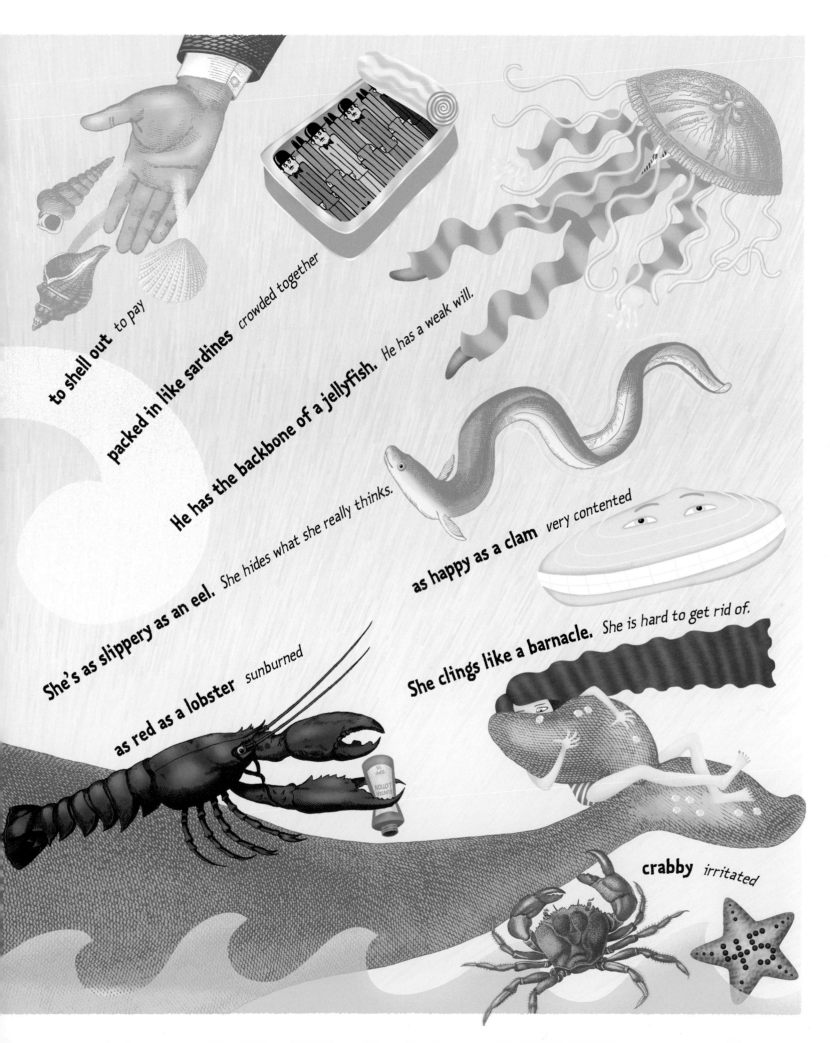

to shell out *to pay*

packed in like sardines *crowded together*

He has the backbone of a jellyfish. *He has a weak will.*

She's as slippery as an eel. *She hides what she really thinks.*

as happy as a clam *very contented*

as red as a lobster *sunburned*

She clings like a barnacle. *She is hard to get rid of.*

crabby *irritated*

**If wishes were horses,
then beggars would ride.**

Desire alone won't make dreams happen.

pet project
favorite project

My crayon broke again!

pet peeve
repeated complaint

teacher's pet
favored student

46

**the black sheep
of the family**

the worst member of the family

WANTED

catcalls
loud yells of disapproval

Boo!
Boo!
Boo!

**She wouldn't
hurt a fly.**
She is gentle.

**The best-laid plans of
mice and men oft go astray.**
Even careful plans can go wrong.

I'll be a monkey's uncle!
I'm amazed!

donkey work
hard physical labor

I'm bullish.
I think stock market prices will go up.

It's driving me batty.
I'm frustrated with it.

I'm as blind as a bat.
My vision is poor.

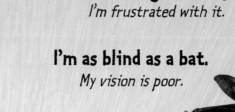

For my feline friends—
Esme, Deli, Abby, Cleo, and Photon
L. L.
And for mine—
Skeezix and Dunkelman
P. S.

Text copyright © 2003 by Loreen Leedy and Pat Street
Illustrations copyright © 2003 by Loreen Leedy
All Rights Reserved
Printed and Bound in November 2019 at Tien Wah Press, Johor Bahru, Johor, Malaysia
14 15 16 17 18 19 20
www.holidayhouse.com

Library of Congress Cataloging-in-Publication Data

Leedy, Loreen.
There's a frog in my throat: 440 animal sayings a little bird told me
by Loreen Leedy and Pat Street; illustrated by Loreen Leedy.—1st ed.
p. cm.
Includes index.
ISBN: 0-8234-1774-3 (hardcover)
ISBN: 0-8234-1819-7 (paperback)

1. English language—Terms and phrases—Juvenile literature.
2. Zoology—Nomenclature (Popular)—Juvenile literature.
3. Animals—Folklore—Juvenile literature.
4. Figures of speech—Juvenile literature. [1. English language—Terms and phrases.
2. Figures of speech. 3. Animals—Folklore.]
I. Street, Pat. II. Title.

PE1583.L39 2003
428.1-dc21   2002068920

ISBN-13: 978-0-8234-1774-2 (hardcover)
ISBN-13: 978-0-8234-1819-0 (paperback)

HOLIDAY HOUSE is registered in the U.S. Patent and Trademark Office

I'm bearish.
I think stock market prices will go down.

48

the tail end
the very end